The Pawsome Pack's Kids' Guide to AI

By Patricia O'Grady

Special Tech Note: This book was developed using the very AI tools described in these pages — proving that big ideas come to life when humans and technology collaborate.

Patricia was the creator, AI was the helper.

Published by **Pawsitively Pawsome Press**
Printed in the United States of America.

ISBN 979-8-9943334-3-3

1st Edition — May 2026

More Adventures Await!

There is a whole world of Pawsome Pack Fun waiting for you! Books, gear, and surprises. Scan the QR code to visit our website and keep exploring with the pack.

www.pawsomepack.fun

✨ Distributed globally via Ingram Content Group and Amazon.

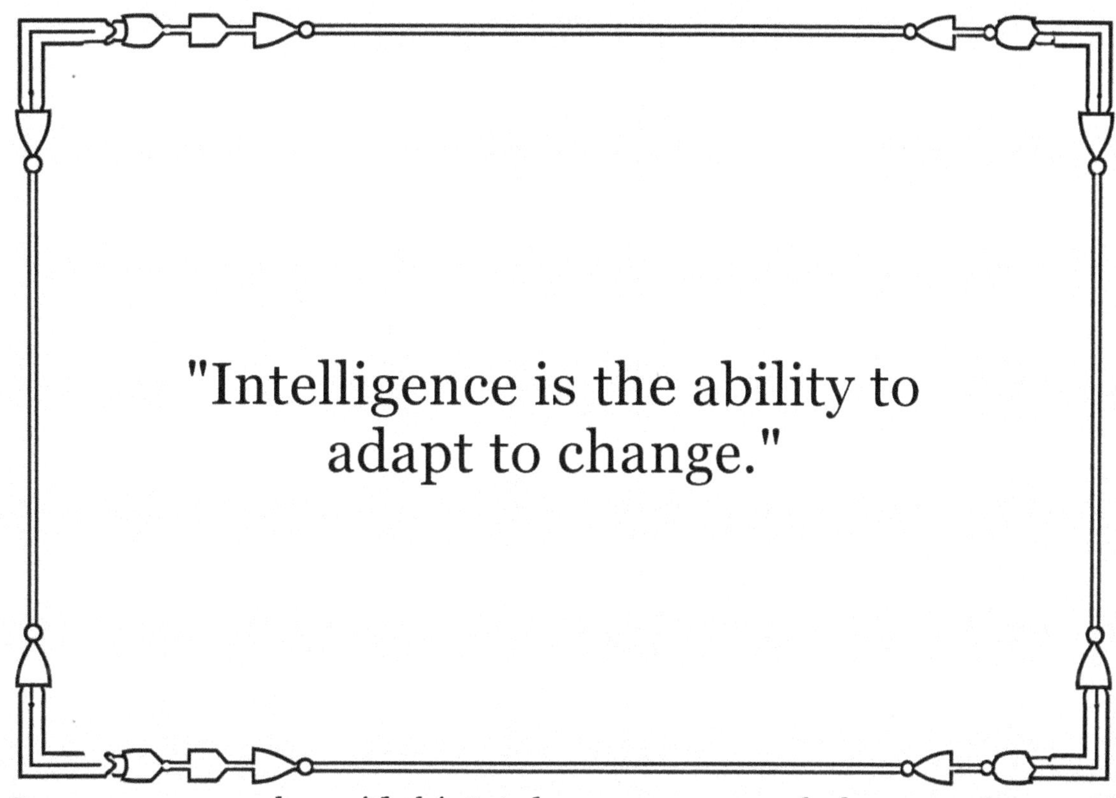

"Intelligence is the ability to
adapt to change."

Can you guess who said this? Ask a grown-up to help you ask an AI!

I am so excited that you have picked my book! AI is an exciting world full of possibilities for those who are willing to embrace the future. By choosing this book, you're already showing that's YOU!

The most important thing to remember when working with AI is — YOU are the creator; AI is the helper! You are going to see this several times throughout the book. You're going to see this a lot in this book, and it really matters! In this book, we discuss **Critical Thinking skills** — it is super important that you work on developing those! Since, you picked this book, I think you are already on a good start to mastering YOUR **Digital Literacy**.

"Digital Literacy" might sound like a big, fancy phrase—but it's actually simple!

Think of **Digital Literacy** as having "internet superpowers." It's more than just knowing how to swipe on a phone or open an app; it's about being smart, safe, and kind whenever you're using technology.

Here are the four main parts of being digitally literate:

- The "How-To" Skills: Knowing how to use your tools. This is like knowing how to type, how to search for a video, or how to save a file so you can find it later.

- The "Truth-Detector": Not everything on the internet is true! A digitally literate person stops and thinks: *"Is this a real fact, or is someone just playing a prank?"* It's like being a detective for information.

- The "Safety-Shield": This is knowing how to keep your private stuff private. You wouldn't give a stranger your house key, right? Digital Literacy means, you don't give out your passwords, home address, last name, age or birthday online.

- The "Kindness-Code": This is how you treat people. Since you can't see someone's face when you're typing, it's easy to forget there's a real person on the other side. Being digitally literate means being a "good digital citizen" and treating people with respect.

In short: It's having the brains to use the tech, instead of letting the tech use you!

I encourage you to explore this book with a parent, grown-ups, and friends. Always ask permission before trying any projects in this book. I bet you all will strike up some amazing conversations together over many of these topics!

Little-known fact! This book started out as a coloring book! There were some MEGA COOL pages to color! Sadly, those pages didn't make the book. BUT the good news is — they DID make the website! Ask a grown-up to visit www.pawsomepack.fun with you and find those pages if you're looking for a little extra book fun! Those pages will be on my website for free.

💚 Patricia!

DON'T FORGET THE SPRINKLES!

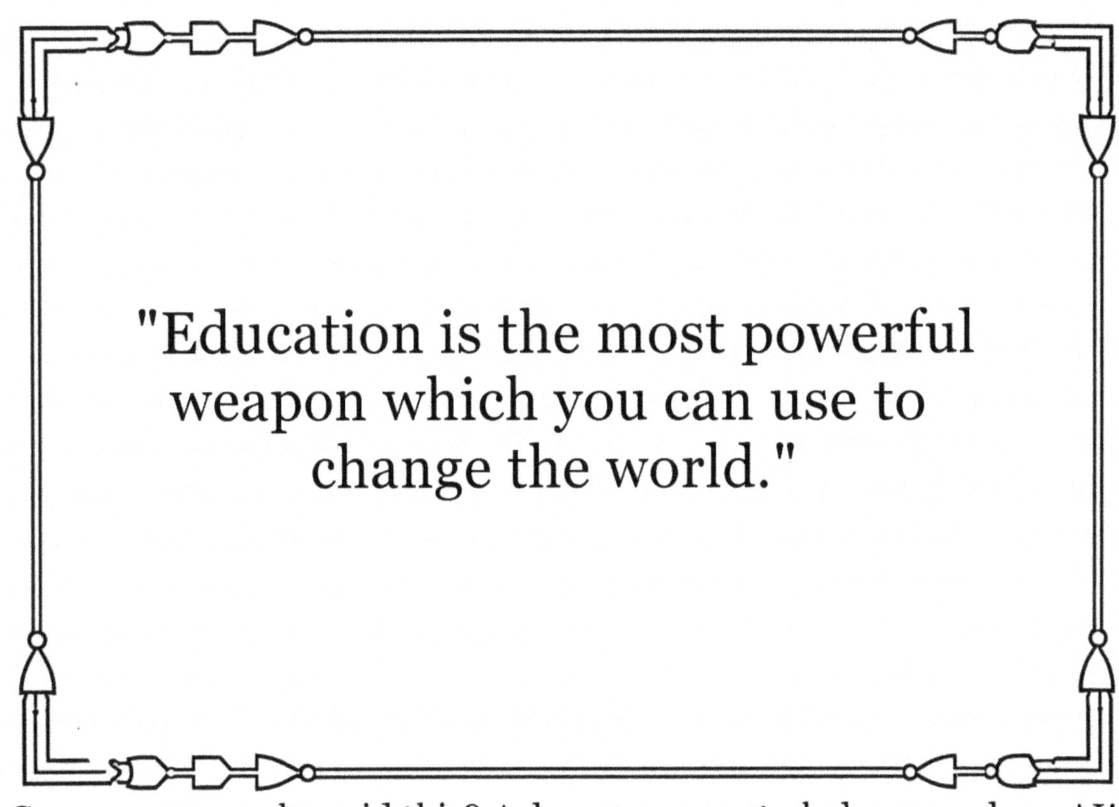

Can you guess who said this? Ask a grown-up to help you ask an AI!

WHAT IS AI?

AI stands for Artificial Intelligence.
It is a smart helper that learns and helps you do cool stuff!

AI can

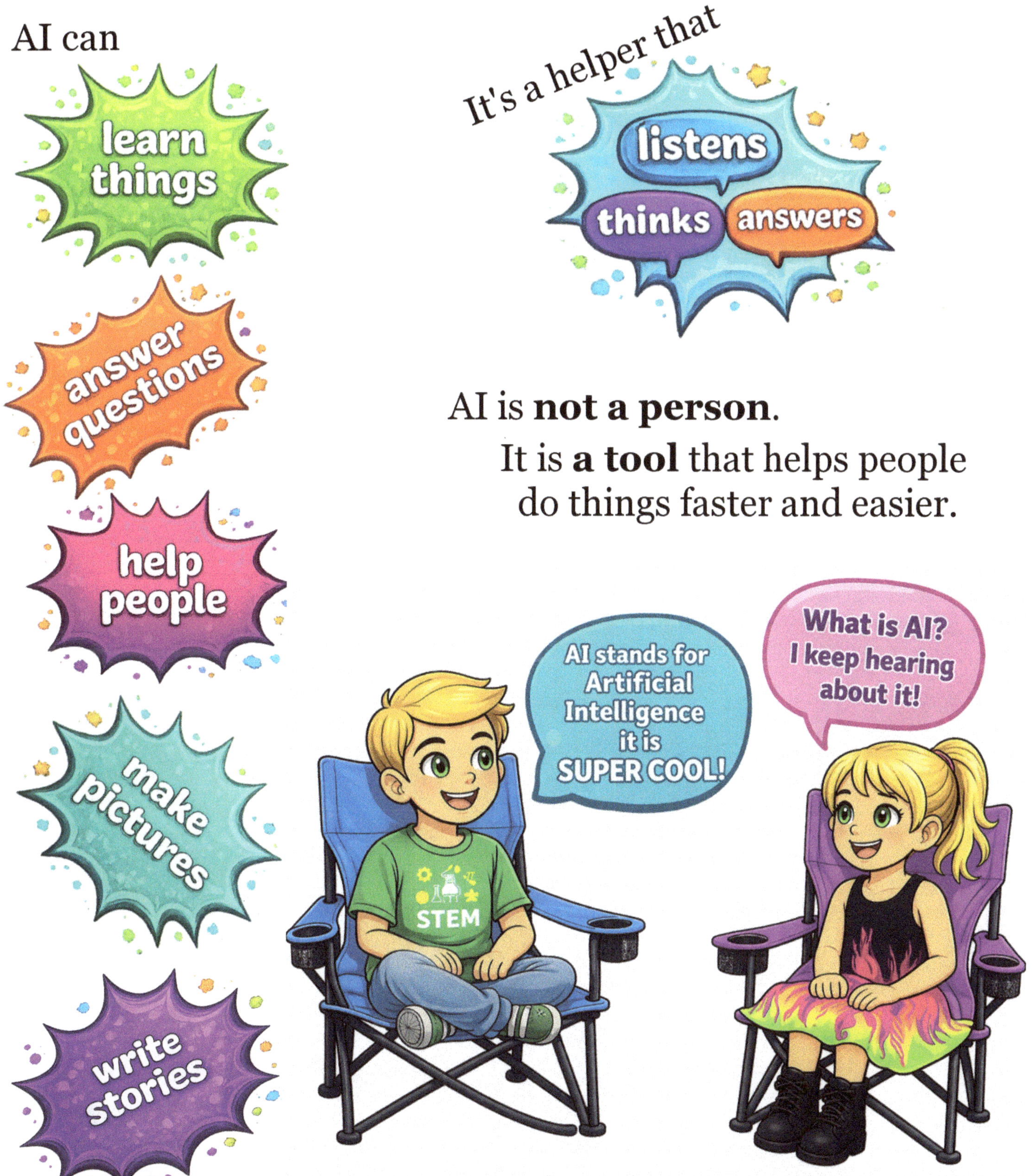

AI is **not a person**.

It is **a tool** that helps people do things faster and easier.

HOW AI LEARNS!
Finding Patterns

 **AI learns by looking at lots of examples.
It finds patterns and groups things that match.
The more it sees, the better it gets.**

This is called pattern recognition / classification.

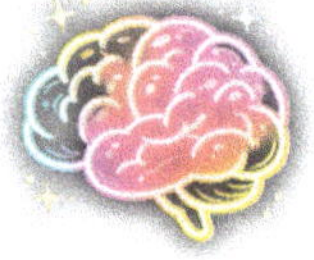 **Inside AI is something called a neural network.
It helps the AI compare examples and
spot patterns, just like our brains do.**

Neural comes from "neuron," like the cells in a brain.

The stars on the chalkboard are called Training Data.
Just like you practice your scales for music or drills for soccer,
an AI needs to "practice" with data to get smart.

**At first AI might not get it right.
It learns by being corrected and retrying.**

Just like we do when we learn!

AI HAS ANSWERS

AI answers questions by using patterns it has learned from lots of examples.

Then it predicts the best answer.

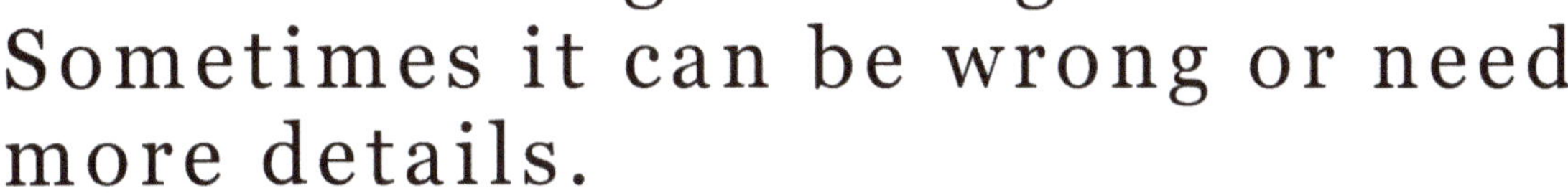

Sometimes it gets it right.
Sometimes it can be wrong or need more details.
AI is not perfect.
If you think the answer might not be right, try asking in a different way.

Sometimes AI is so eager to give you an answer that it might make one up.
This is called a **hallucination**.

Critical Thinking and Digital Literacy are key!

Don't just accept what you are told.
Check to make sure it's correct.

Ask a grown-up to help you look up **Evaluate** and **Iterate** in a dictionary.

AI HELPS PEOPLE!

AI is a tool that helps people do things faster and easier. You can ask AI questions. It gives you ideas, steps, or answers to help you get started.

Sometimes people use AI to:

- Plan projects
- Learn new things
- Solve problems
- Get creative ideas

Dagen and Vanya asked AI how to make a lava lamp experiment! It gave them a list of materials and simple steps to follow. That helped them get started quickly.

AI helps people — but you are the thinker!

Vanya! Let's have him help us make a lava lamp!

LETS MAKE THIS!

What you need:

- » Clear glass
- » Ice cubes
- » Fruit-flavored drink powder (any color)
- » Clear, carbonated soda (like lemon-lime soda)
- » Spoon

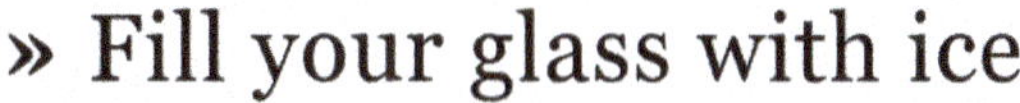

Steps:

- » Fill your glass with ice
- » Add the fruit drink powder
- » Pour in a little water and stir
- » Slowly add the clear soda
- » Watch the bubbles move the color!

What's happening?

This is called **buoyancy**.
Gas bubbles are lighter than the liquid, so they rise up and carry the color with them.

Want More Colors?

The steps above will create **ONE** main color for your lava lamp.

To make multiple colors, try this:

- » Use 2-3 different colored drink powders
- » Add each color separately
  - • Add 1 color, then right away add another color
  - • Don't stir — let the bubbles do the work
- » Pour slowly

 **Ask a grown-up to help.**
They need a little fun too!

WHAT DID WE LEARN?

You tested it, watched it, and learned from it!

That's STEM!

Want to color this page? It's available for free at www.pawsomepack.fun

THE AI BREAKDOWN

Artificial Narrow Intelligence

ANI is really good at doing one specific thing: it can answer questions, make pictures, or help you with a task. It just can't do everything like a human can. ANI only knows how to do the job it was trained for — like having one special superpower instead of many.

Artificial General Intelligence

AGI can learn and do many different things, like a human can. Instead of being good at only one task, AGI understands new problems, think through them, and help with lots of different kinds of work. It would be more flexible and able to learn new skills, not just stick to one job.

Artificial Super Intelligence

ASI is smarter than humans at almost everything. It could learn faster, solve problems better, and come up with ideas we might not even think of. ASI doesn't exist right now, but it's something people imagine for the future.

Above are the 3 basic types of AI — but there are more! Try asking your AI to teach you about them. Start your prompt "Explain to me like I am ____ years old (so AI knows how to answer you) what is:

Reactive Machine AI | Limited Memory AI | Theory of Mind AI | Self Aware AI

Want to dig even deeper? You can even ask:
Explain to me the difference in <u>THIS AI</u> versus <u>THIS AI</u>.

~ This is best done with an adult nearby! ~

SPOTLIGHT ON ANI

ANI is like a super-specialist. It's incredibly smart at doing **one or two things**—like playing your favorite song, telling you the weather, or setting a timer for cookies.

But because it's "Narrow," it doesn't know everything! It doesn't know how to play fetch, it doesn't know how to dream, and it definitely hasn't learned "Chihuahua" yet.

THE BIG TAKEAWAY

Most of the AI we use today—from the videos you watch to the maps in a car—is **ANI**.

It's a great helper, but it still needs **YOU** to tell it what to do!

EVERYDAY ANI
PUZZLE HINTS
GOOGLE HOME
MATH-SOLVING APPS
EMAIL SPAM FILTERS
PRICE TRACKING / DEAL ALERTS
AMAZON "YOU MIGHT ALSO LIKE"
TIKTOK / INSTAGRAM FEEDS
YOUTUBE "UP NEXT" VIDEOS
FINGERPRINT UNLOCK
NEXT WORD SUGGESTIONS
GOOGLE ASSISTANT
GAME DIFFICULTY ADJUSTING TO YOUR SKILL
FRAUD DETECTION ON CREDIT CARDS
AI TUTORS / HOMEWORK HELPERS
TRAFFIC PREDICTION (REROUTING YOU)
AUTOCORRECT WHEN YOU TYPE
ALEXA
ANI
SIRI
PARKING APPS SHOWING OPEN SPOTS
FACE UNLOCK
SPAM CALL & SPAM TEXT FILTERS
NETFLIX MOVIE SUGGESTIONS
UBER / LYFT MATCHING DRIVERS
PRODUCT RECOMMENDATIONS ON WEBSITES
SMART LIGHTS (VOICE OR SCHEDULE CONTROLLED)
ROBOT VACUUMS
VOICE ASSISTANTS (SIRI, ALEXA, GOOGLE ASSISTANT)
PREDICTIVE TEXT ("NEXT WORD" SUGGESTIONS)
CHESS/COMPUTER OPPONENTS
SPOTIFY / APPLE MUSIC RECOMMENDATIONS
GOOGLE MAPS DIRECTIONS
NPCS (NON-PLAYER CHARACTERS IN GAMES)

AI MAKES PICTURES

Think of AI like a student who has looked at lots of sketches, paintings, and photos. AI doesn't copy them; instead, AI learns the **patterns** of how things look: like how a sunset has warm colors or how a dog has four legs and a tail. Once it knows these patterns, AI uses them to "imagine" a brand-new picture for you.

AI knows exactly what makes a 'cat' look like a 'cat' so it can draw one from scratch whenever you ask!

You are still the creator — AI is just the helper.

👉 Prompt!

A **prompt** is just a fancy word for "instructions." When you tell an AI exactly what you want it to draw, — like "A jungle scene" — you are giving AI a **prompt**! The more details you give, the better AI can find the right pattern to use.

Simple prompt

A MORE DETAILED PROMPT

Want to color this page? It's available for free at www.pawsomepack.fun

ASK YOUR AI!

This will be a super fun thing to do!
You're going to chat with your AI!
BUT! In order to do this, you need to ask a grown-up to hang out with you for a little bit while you talk to your AI!

You remember what **Prompts** are right? If not, go back a few pages and check! Start each of your **prompts** like this:
"Explain to me like I am _____ years old..."
then ask your question. This helps AI know how to word answers for you.

» Give me 5 cool space facts!

» What's a great snack I can make?

» What's the difference in a hurricane versus a tsunami?

» What was the biggest dinosaur?

» What was the most dangerous dinosaur?

» How can I make a dog happy?

» What is the most popular sport?

» Can you help me plan a super fun day?

» What's the oldest animal in the world?

» Write me a funny story about a ninja cat!

» Draw me a picture of a crazy cool cartoon axolotl.

Why a grown-up? Remember, AI is NOT always right.
A grown-up can help you check if the information is accurate.
You are still working on your **critical thinking** skills.
In case AI **hallucinates**, they can help you **Evaluate** and **Iterate**.
Look at you! Already knowing all these crazy big technical terms!

AI WRITES STORIES!

Imagine someone who has read almost every book in the world! They don't know stories the way we do, but they recognize patterns in how sentences are built. When we tell them to write a story, they predict which words should come next to make the story! That's AI!

AI is our creative partner. It helps us get past those "writer's block" moments by suggesting names, settings, or wild plot twists! We are still the Lead Authors — AI just helps us get the ideas out of our head and onto the page!

Pro Tip! The more details you give, the better the story!

McTuberson: The Worst Ninja at Lake Hubbardson

McTuberson was supposed to be a ninja. That was the problem.

At the dojo near Lake Hubbardson, every cat trained to be fast, silent, and precise. They could leap between trees without a sound, land perfectly on narrow beams, and disappear into shadows like they were never there.

McTuberson could not do any of those things.
McTuberson was… built differently.
He wasn't exactly fat, but he was definitely rounder than the other cats. When he ran, he bounced a little. When he jumped, he usually landed… eventually.

And when he tried to be quiet?
Well.
Let's just say the birds always knew he was coming.

"Again," said Master Whiskerdoom.
McTuberson stood at the edge of a practice beam. It was only a few inches off the ground. Super easy.

For everyone else.

He stepped up, focused hard, and started walking.
One step.
Two steps.
He smiled. This was going well.
Then his back paw slipped.
His front paw panicked.
His tail tried to help.
It did not help.

McTuberson landed on the ground with a soft grunt.

From the side, another student whispered, "How is he still here?"

"I heard he failed sneaking past a sleeping turtle," someone else said.

"It woke up," McTuberson mumbled. "It was a very alert turtle."

Here's the thing nobody really knew.
McTuberson didn't even want to be a ninja.
Not really.
What he really wanted was to be an ice cream man.

Every night after training, McTuberson would roll his little wooden cart down to the edge of Lake Hubbardson.
The cart was kind of a mess.
One wheel squeaked loudly.
One wheel tilted slightly inward. And the bell on top rang whenever it felt like it.

Jingle... jingle...

"I'll fix that someday," McTuberson always said.

Inside the cart, he practiced.
Scooping imaginary ice cream.
Perfect round scoops.
Careful balance.
Gentle placement on cones.
It was the one thing he didn't mess up.

"Two scoops of Tuna Twist!" he'd say to no one.
"Extra Salmon Swirl!"
He even bowed after serving.

Which made no sense, but it felt right.

One evening, as the sun went down over the lake, Master Whiskerdoom
walked up behind him.
"You are practicing," the master said.
McTuberson jumped.
The bell rang.

JINGLE.
"Yep," McTuberson said quickly. "Practicing... ninja stuff."
The master looked at the cart.
Then at McTuberson.
"...Ice cream?" he asked.

"...Advanced ninja training," McTuberson said.
The master didn't argue.

That night, everything changed.
A group of raccoon bandits had been spotted sneaking toward the dojo's
storage building.

"They're after supplies," said Master Whiskerdoom. "We move quietly."

Every ninja nodded.
They spread out into the darkness.
Silent.
Focused.
Invisible.
Then—

CRASH.

Everyone froze.
McTuberson had tripped over his own cart.
The bell went wild.
JINGLE JANGLE JINGLE.

Master Whiskerdoom slowly turned his head.
"...Try to be less you," he said.

"I'll try," McTuberson whispered.

The raccoons were close now, creeping toward the building.
Everything depended on timing.
Stealth.
Control.
McTuberson stepped forward.
Carefully.
Very carefully.
He almost made it three steps.

Then he stepped on a loose rock.
Slipped.
Flipped.
Rolled downhill.
"AHHHH—!"

And slammed directly into the group of raccoons.

Total chaos.
Raccoons yelling.
McTuberson spinning.
A sack of supplies flying through the air.
Someone dropped a lantern.
Another raccoon tripped trying to catch it.

Everything went completely out of control in about three seconds.

McTuberson, panicking, grabbed the nearest thing—which turned out to be the stolen supplies—and somehow kicked it away from the raccoons.

The raccoons looked at each other.
Looked at McTuberson.
And ran.
Fast.

Silence returned.
Slowly.

The other ninjas stepped out from hiding.
No one spoke for a moment.
McTuberson lay on his back, blinking up at the sky.
"...Did I ruin it?" he asked.

Master Whiskerdoom looked at the untouched supplies.
Then at the empty forest.
Then back at McTuberson.
"...No," he said.
"You ruined the plan," he added.
"...But you solved the problem."

The next morning, McTuberson stood in front of the dojo.
Nervous.
Master Whiskerdoom stepped forward.

"You are not a good ninja," he said plainly.

McTuberson nodded.
"I know."
"You are loud."
"Yep."
"You fall down a lot."
"...Also yep."
The master paused.

"But you do not give up. And you care about doing things right."

McTuberson blinked.
"That matters," the master said.

He pointed toward the lake.
Toward the cart.

"You should follow the path you are actually good
at."

HOW DID WE DO THAT?

A story prompt example

> Write a fun story about a clumsy ninja frog named (NAME) who lives near (PLACE). He is very bad at being a ninja because he always trips and makes noise. His real dream is to be a Hot Dog Vendor. One day, he accidentally saves the day in a silly way. In the end, he decides to follow his dream and sell Hot Dogs. Make the story funny.

PROMPTS!

You remember we discussed **Prompts**? They are what you tell an AI to turn your wildest ideas into reality. It's like having a magic wand, but you have to use your words to wave it!

Don't forget the sprinkles!

Think of a basic prompt like a plain scoop of vanilla ice cream. It's good, but it's a little bit boring, right?

Details are the sprinkles on top! the more "sprinkles" you add to your **prompt**,

An image prompt example

> Draw a simple cartoon of a chubby ninja frog sneaking past a sleeping sloth.
>
> Make it look like a kids coloring book. Use thick black lines and bright colors.
>
> The character is a chubby ninja Frog with one pink eye and one teal eye.

the more flavorful and unique your result becomes. Without them, the AI has to guess what you like. With them, you create a masterpiece!

NOW YOU'RE COOKIN' WITH AI!

Vanya's Crispy Rainbow Treats!

- ⭐ 1/2 cup butter
- ⭐ 8 cups marshmallows (white)
- ⭐ 2 cups marshmallows (🌈 colored)
- ⭐ 10 cups crisped rice cereal

🥄 Melt butter in a large saucepan over low heat.

🥄 Add 8 cups white marshmallows and stir until melted.

🥄 Once melted, turn off the heat and fold in the cereal.

❗ **Never add colored marshmallows while the pot is still on the heat.**

🥄 Wait 30 seconds for the temperature to drop, then fold in the colored marshmallows.

Don't over-stir! The more you stir, the more the heat breaks down the marshmallows. Fold gently to distribute them.

When you put the mixture into a 9"x13" pan, **don't pack it down hard**. Use a piece of buttered parchment paper or a greased spatula to lightly pat them down.

If you press too hard, you'll squish the colored marshmallows and force the colors to run into the cereal.

💕 Grab a grown-up to have them help you with this! They taste much sweeter when cooked with love! 💕

What an incredible day! Dagen and Vanya learned that AI isn't just about computers and code—it's a tool that helps our wildest ideas come to life.

From imagining clumsy ninja cats to baking the perfect batch of rainbow treats, they discovered that the real "magic" comes from the person using the tool.

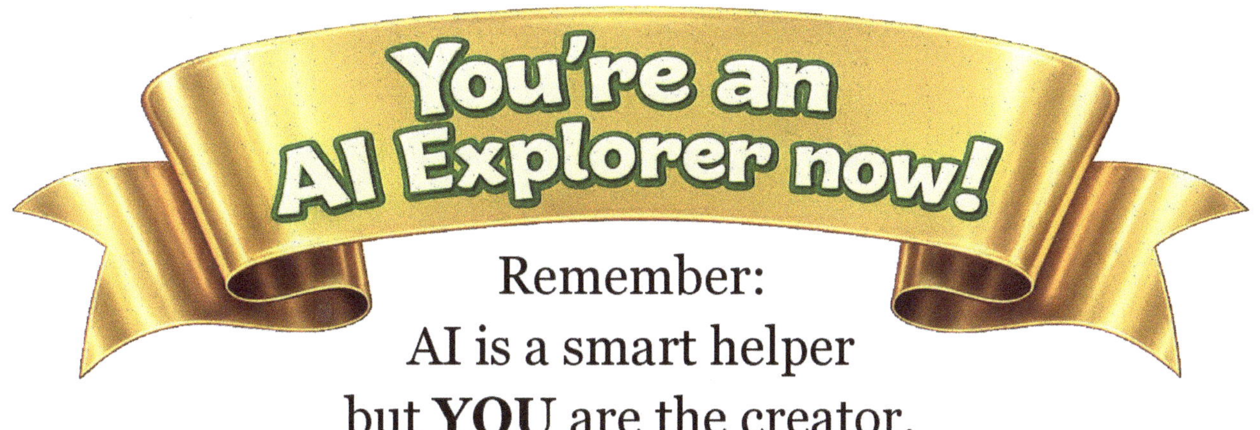

Remember:
AI is a smart helper
but **YOU** are the creator.

Keep asking questions, keep being curious, and always remember to add your own "sprinkles" to everything you do.

WHERE THE ADVENTURE CONTINUES!

OUR BOOKS

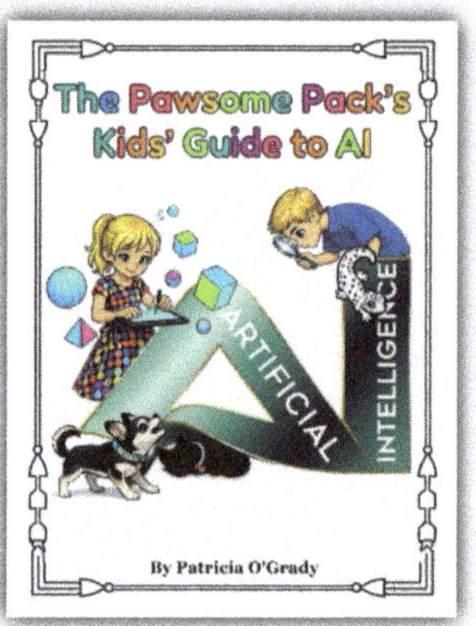

✨ Distributed globally via Ingram Content Group and Amazon.
PAWSOMEPACK.FUN/PAWSOME-DISTRIBUTION

TO STAY UP TO DATE WITH PAWSITIVELY PAWSOME PRESS AND THE PAWSOME PACK, VISIT:

PAWSOMEPACK.FUN

THERE YOU'LL FIND FREE COLORING AND ACTIVITY PAGES, OUR BOOKS, SUPER COOL "BUSSIN" SWAG, AND EVEN PAWSOME PACK JAMZ TO ROCK OUT TO!

KEEP THE FUN GOING!
SCAN TO VISIT
OUR SITE!